BUZZ ABOUT
Bees

by KARI-LYNN WINTERS

Fitzhenry & Whiteside

Published in Canada by Fitzhenry & Whiteside, 195 Allstate Parkway, Markham, Ontario L3R 4T8

Published in the United States by Fitzhenry & Whiteside, 311 Washington Street, Brighton, Massachusetts 02135

http://www.fitzhenry.ca
godwit@fitzhenry.ca

10 9 8 7 6 5 4 3 2 1

Library and Archives Canada Cataloguing in Publication

Winters, Kari-Lynn, 1969-
        Buzz about bees / Kari-Lynn Winters.
Includes index.
ISBN 978-1-55455-202-3
1. Bees—Juvenile literature. 2. Honey—Juvenile literature.
I. Title.
QL565.2.W55 2012   j595.79'9   C2012-906471-8

Publisher Cataloging-in-Publication Data (U.S.)
Winters, Kari-Lynn.
  Buzz about bees / Kari-Lynn Winters.
[48] p. : col. photos. ; cm.
Includes index. Summary: An in-depth look at the history and social structure of and science behind the world of bees and honey.
ISBN: 978-1-55455-202-3
1. Bees - Juvenile literature. 2. Honeybee - Juvenile literature.
I. Title. 595.79/9 dc23   QL565.2. W5684 2012

Fitzhenry & Whiteside acknowledges with thanks the Canada Council for the Arts, and the Ontario Arts Council for their support of our publishing program. We acknowledge the financial support of the Government of Canada through the Canada Book Fund (CBF) for our publishing activities.

Cover and interior design by John Luckhurst Graphic Design
Cover image courtesy of David Wysotski (Allure Illustrations)

Printed by Friesens in Altona, MB, Canada in March 2013.
Job #75217

The publisher shall not be liable for injuries or damage caused by conducting activities in this book. Readers are cautioned to follow instructions carefully and to seek adult supervision where noted.

CONTENTS

Dedication

To Rachel Winters, who inspired us to keep our backyard "wild," thus inviting diverse bees to forage and keep our garden pollinated.

Acknowledgements

I would like to acknowledge the contributions of many people who added to the contents of this book and made it possible. To the bee lovers and researchers who vetted the book and helped me better understand the lives of bees, including Bubbees Honey, Clovermead Adventure Farm, Douglas Karrow, David Wysotski, Adrienne Mason and the staff at KNOW Magazine, Glen and Gwen McMullen, Tom Onuferko, Laurence Packer, Miriam Richards, Jacqui Shields, Paul and Maude Stephany, Jess Vickruck, and Andrea Wilson and the staff at the Ball's Falls Conservation Area. Thanks also to Cathy Sandusky, Christie Harkin, Solange Messier, Cheryl Chen, and all of the others at Fitzhenry & Whiteside who believed in this project and put the pieces together to make it happen. I also appreciate the writers who diligently looked over sections of the manuscript, including Sandra Bosacki, Michelle McGinn, Snezana Ratkovic, Tiffany Stone, and Jonah Winters. Finally, I would also like to acknowledge the book's models, including Christie, Liam, McKenna, Jase, and Cooper.

BEE-LIEVE IT OR NOT, BEES ARE SOMETHING TO BUZZ ABOUT

True or False?

1. Bees are important. They help keep us healthy.

2. All bees have stingers.

3. Honeybees are native to North America.

4. In some countries, people eat bees.

5. Bees have been admired by people for thousands of years.

6. Honey can be used as a natural medicine.

7. In recent years, some species of bees have gone extinct.

8. Yellow jackets are bees.

9. Making small changes in your environment can help bees thrive.

10. There is a lot to know about bees.

Answer Key: 1-T, 2-F, 3-F, 4-T, 5-T, 6-T, 7-T, 8-F, 9-T, 10-T.
Read through the book to find out more interesting facts about bees.

CHAPTER 1

BEE-N THERE, DONE THAT

Bees have been admired throughout history and are still cherished today. Cave paintings from around 13,000 BCE found in Africa, Europe, Asia, and Australia show bees painted near other sacred animals. These "petroglyphs" were painted with pigments and animal fat onto caves and temples, but their purpose is not known. Perhaps their creators used these images to communicate with or warn other nomads, to pass on myths and traditions, or during rituals and religious ceremonies. Regardless, the fact that the bees are represented at all demonstrates their importance within these hunter-gatherer societies.

JOB POSTING...

HONEY HUNTERS WANTED

If you lived during pre-historic times would you have wanted to be a **honey hunter**? Answer these questions with either **YES** or **NO** to find out.

1. Do you like the sound of buzzing bees?
2. Would you be willing to climb great heights on a flimsy ladder made from grass and weeds?
3. Do you have experience holding a flame torch and sharp knife while balancing on a wobbly, tall ladder?
4. Could you hold onto the underside of an extremely high cliff for several minutes if your ladder happened to collapse?
5. Would you remain still and steady on your ladder (or clinging to the underside of a cliff) while being swarmed by hundreds of protective bees defending their nests?
6. Do you enjoy painful bee stings?

If you answered **NO** to any of the above questions, perhaps the honey-hunter job is not for you.

Cave paintings demonstrate how treacherous these honey hunts must have been. Daring hunters endured troublesome heights, unsafe ladders, and piercing stings simply to satisfy their sweet-tooth cravings. With only primitive tools—a grass ladder, a torch, and a knife—they robbed nests in search of delicious, tangy honey.

BEE-ing Worthy of Royal Status

Over 5,000 years ago Egyptian pharaohs (ancient rulers) used a formal writing system called **hieroglyphics**. Hieroglyphs consisted of combinations of symbols and letters engraved or painted onto pottery, ivory tags, ancient tombs, and sacred temples. It is interesting to note that the bee hieroglyph shown here (on right) was a royal symbol representing "the domain of the pharaoh."

People from ancient Greece thought highly of bees. In fact, bees were so important that the Greeks put a symbol of the bee on one of their coins.

Take Your Medicine: Drink Your Honey

For thousands of years humans have recognized the medicinal uses of honey or **mead** (fermented honey water). These liquids were known to have natural anti-biotic, antifungal, and anti-inflammatory properties. People used these sweet liquids to clean sores, loosen phlegm, ward off infections, relieve constipation, reduce diarrhea, eliminate allergies and acne outbreaks, cure coughs and sore throats, and numb menstrual cramps. In medieval times, people would soak bandages in honey in order to reduce joint swelling and cure cataracts. Some of these honey cures continue to be used for health purposes today. For example, honey is a primary ingredient in several cough syrups and drops. And when a person has laryngitis (an inflamed larynx), a common home remedy might be ginger tea sweetened by honey or a warm honey/lemon gargle.

Recipe for Soothing a STING-ing Throat
A Honey/Lemon Gargle

Ingredients:

1   cup (235 ml) of warm water (soothes the throat)
½   squeezed lemon (reduces swelling)
1   teaspoon (5 ml) of honey (has antibacterial properties and sweetens the liquid)
¼   teaspoon (1.25 ml) of salt (kills germs)

Directions:

1. Mix ingredients in a cup.
2. Gargle. Do not swallow.
3. Spit it out.
4. Repeat as needed.

In addition to honey, bees provide other valuable products. **Beeswax** *continues to be used in cosmetics, candles, soaps, and lip balms.* **Propolis**, *a tree resin collected by bees, is known to treat gum infections and minor burns. Bee pollen is used to increase energy and aid in digestion.*

BEESWAX

CHAPTER 2

THE WHOLE BALL OF WAX

A bee's body is divided into three distinct sections: the head, the **thorax**, and the abdomen. On their heads are eyes, antennae, a tongue, and specialized mouthparts.

The thorax's main purpose is transportation—both of pollen and for the bee itself. It is also considered to be the muscle centre of the bee because it is where the muscles used for flight and locomotion are found. The bee's six legs and four wings are attached to its thorax.

The honeybee's abdomen houses most of its digestive and reproductive internal organs, including its honey crop (also called its honey stomach), intestine, and ovaries. On the outside, seven hardened plates connected by membranes protect the abdomen. For some bees—those that build wax structures— these plates expand when the stomach is full of nectar or when the bee secretes flakes of beeswax.

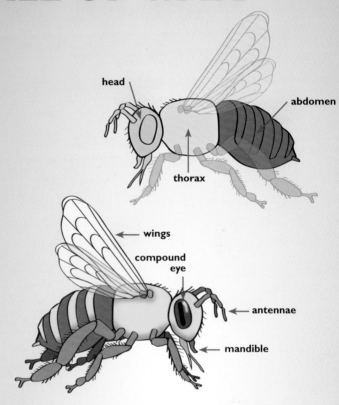

Female honeybees have six hardened plates on the outside of their abdomens, while males have seven.

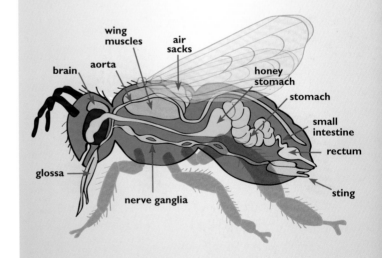

UnBEE-lievable Body Parts

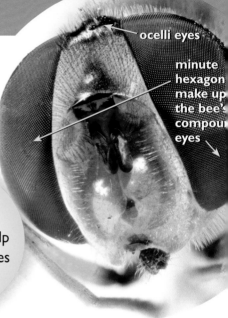

ocelli eyes

minute hexagon make up the bee's compound eyes

Eyes

Bees have five eyes. Two are hairy **compound eyes** that perceive airflow, detect colours, and spot movement. Under a microscope one can see that these compound eyes are made up of approximately 6,900 hexagons, which help the bee see all around its body. Three smaller eyes called **ocelli** are found between the bee's compound eyes. Scientists believe these more primitive eyes detect light intensity.

Nocturnal bees have much larger ocelli to help detect light changes in darkness.

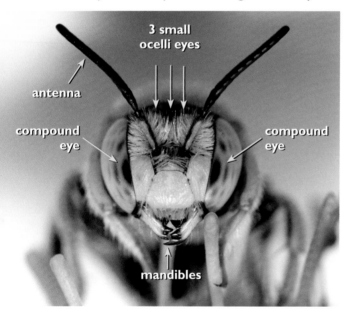

3 small ocelli eyes

antenna

compound eye

compound eye

mandibles

Antennae

Two antennae set into sockets below the eyes help bees detect and adapt to their surroundings. With these antennae they can feel changes in the weather, smell **pheromones** (chemical signals sent by other bees), identify hive intruders, and find food sources. Under a microscope these antennae look like segmented worms covered with craters and bristly hairs.

Mouthparts

In order to shape their nests, eat pollen, and bite off or manipulate wood, plant resins, and wax, bees need large jaws, called mandibles. Bees also have long, straw-like tongues called proboscises. The **proboscis** is used to sip nectar from flowers and to feed their larvae.

Some bees have long tongues (mining bees) and others have short tongues (plasterer bees). The types of tongues they have determine what types of pollen they gather. Long-tongued bees typically like deeper flowers and short-tongued bees prefer flowers that are more shallow.

Stingers

Most bees are not aggressive. However, if you block a nest, trap or hurt a bee, or move too fast, you may receive a painful, venomous sting from a female—as only females have stingers.

Bees with barbed or hooked stingers are usually cautious about who or what they sting; when a bee with this type of stinger stings its victim, the bee will most likely die. The stinger can't be removed without rupturing the bee's abdomen.

BEE-ware! A honeybee's stinger is barbed—more like a screw than a nail.

Bee stings are not usually fatal. Mostly they cause redness, rashes, and/or discomfort. However, some people are allergic to the venomous stings, and their reactions can be more severe. They can lose consciousness or even die without medical intervention. People who are allergic to bee stings should carry an EpiPen™ at all times in order to manage any allergy emergencies.

A desert biologist named Justin Schmidt has taken on the job of getting stung by bees (and other insects) around the world so that he can create a pain index. Schmidt describes a sting from a sweat bee as light—"a tiny spark." A honeybee sting is more painful. It is described as a "match head that…burns your skin."

How to Use an EpiPen™

1. Remove the EpiPen from the carrier case.
2. Form a fist around the EpiPen. Ensure that the needle end is pointing downward.
3. Pull off the safety-release cap.
4. Place needle end against outer mid-thigh (it will pierce through clothing).
5. Swing arm so that the needle end embeds into the thigh (a click will be heard).
6. Hold the EpiPen firmly in place for 10 seconds.
7. Remove EpiPen. Do not touch the needle.
8. Massage the affected area.
9. Seek medical attention.
10. Give the used EpiPen to the emergency responders to ensure safe disposal.

Legs

Bees, like all insects, have six legs. They use their legs to claw and scrape trees and flowers, dig out and build their nests or hives, clean themselves and their queens, and carry pollen. Some bees, such as the bumblebee and the honeybee, have concave regions on their broad hind legs called **pollen baskets**.

At the tips of their legs, bees have suction cups and sensitive hairs. The suction cups help them climb vertical surfaces such as walls or fences. The sensitive hairs help them "taste" their environments.

Wings

Powered by nectar, bees use their powerful wing muscles for flight. On their thoraxes are two pairs of wings that can be hooked together. The average bee flaps its wings 200 cycles per second, allowing it to fly up to 14 miles/hour (24 km/hour)—that's as fast as most dogs can run!

In addition to flying forward, bees have the ability to fly backwards and sideways.

forewing

hooks   fold

hindwing

pollen basket

tibia

femur

basitarsus

tarsi

pollen basket

Classifying Bee Bodies

Bees belong to the superfamily *Anthophila* (synonym: *apoidea*). The name comes from "flower bloom" (*anth*) and "to love" (*phila*). Bees do love flowers! A bee's main food sources, nectar and pollen, come from the blooms of flowers.

A single bee can travel to nearly a thousand flowers each day.

There are seven classifications, or families, of bees in the superfamily *Anthophila*. Each is distinguished by its DNA and its physical and social characteristics.

Scientific (family name)	Examples (common names)	Characteristics	Places They May Live
andrenidae	• Mining bees • Passionflower bees	• two ridges (called subantennal sutures) on each side of the face—below the antennae • large heads to burrow in the soil, where they nest • short, pointed tongues • most species in this family are solitary • some species are nocturnal	• Worldwide (except Antarctica and Australia)
apidae	• Honeybees • Carpenter bees • Bumblebees • Stingless bees • Digger bees	• long tongues • transport pollen with hind legs, either pushing it onto stiff hairs called **scopa** or filling pollen baskets (smooth concave areas fringed by stiff hairs) • some are social (e.g., honeybees) and others are solitary (e.g., digger bees)	• Worldwide except Antarctica (though some, like the honeybee, are not native to the North American habitat)
colletidae	• Masked bees • Plasterer bees	• broad tongues with two lobes • short mouthparts • able to secrete a clear substance to line their nests • slender bodies • less than 10mm long • nest in plant stems, or existing holes in wood	• Primarily Australia and South America

continued on next page

Digger Bees

Bees dig holes. A digger bee can dig a hole 6.5 ft (2m) deep, moving soil that is five hundred times its weight. That's like an average man putting two loaded transport trucks on his back.

13

Scientific (family name)	Examples (common names)	Characteristics	Places They May Live
halictidae	• Sweat bees • Alkali bees	• can be metallic in appearance • most species in this family are solitary, while others are social • nest in soil	• Worldwide (except Antarctica and Australia)
megachilidae	• Leafcutter bees • Orchard mason bees • Carder bees	• carry pollen on their abdomens rather than with their hind legs • solitary • bite off pieces of leaves or plant resins to line and construct nests • nest in soil, wood, or hollow plant stems	• Worldwide (except Antarctica and Australia)
melittidae	• Melittid bees	• shaggy pollen apparatuses • collect floral oils to feed their babies • nest in soil or wood	• Worldwide (except Antarctica, Australia, and South America)
stenotritidae	• No common names	• large • furry • short tongues with two lobes • nest in soil	Australia

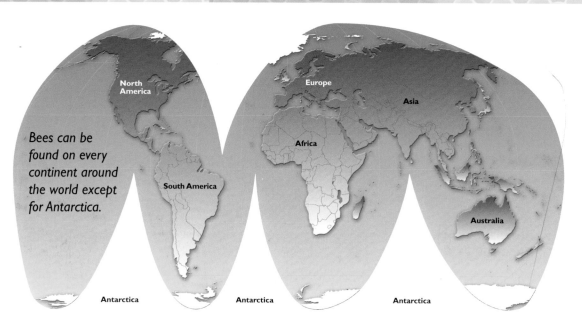

Bees can be found on every continent around the world except for Antarctica.

North America

South America

Antarctica

Europe

Asia

Africa

Antarctica

Australia

Antarctica

To BEE or Not to BEE

What are the differences between bees and wasps? Although they are often confused, there are differences.

Bees use proboscises to sip nectar

pollen basket

Wasps do not have pollen baskets

Honeybees

- Sip nectar and eat pollen
- Covered with tan-brown hairs
- Have stiff hairs and pollen baskets on their hind legs
- Gentle
- Stingers are barbed. Many bee species can only sting once and then they will die

Yellow Jackets

- Eat other insects, waste, and overripe fruit
- Do not have pollen baskets on their slim, long hind legs
- Aggressive
- Stingers are smooth. Yellow-jacket wasps can sting repeatedly without dying

CHAPTER 3

BEE-ING TOGETHER

Social Bees

Social bees live in colonies where they work together in order to survive. Some of these social bees have sophisticated sensory communication systems: beyond just seeing one another, they use their senses of smell, hearing, and touch to warn each other about dangers, to assign and assume roles in the hive, and to share knowledge about where yummy food sources are located.

Some bees live together, but are not considered social bees. True social bees are defined by three criteria:

1. The bees work together to take care of the babies.
2. Baby bees live long enough to help their mother take care of their siblings.
3. Only a few of the bees lay the eggs.

NESTS or HIVES

Colonies of honeybees live together in wax homes. If the home is a natural beehive, like in a hole in a tree, it's called a nest. If the home is built by people or given to domesticated bees, it's called a hive.

Apiaries (colonies that are managed by beekeepers) use wooden boxes, pottery vessels, and woven straw baskets to help bees build their beehives. Worker honeybees, for example, use these homes to raise their babies and to store food.

In the wild, nests are natural structures that can be found in trees, old logs, or rock crevices. Some nests are difficult to find.

Whether wild or domestic, honeybees use wax that is produced by wax glands in their abdomens. They chew and mould the wax into perfect hexagon cells. This mass of cells that is found inside their nest or hive is called a honeycomb. Honeycombs are very strong.

This man-made bees' home is called a hive.

A bees' home in the wild, like this tree, is called a nest.

Bees work tirelessly to build a honeycomb like this one.

Queens are labelled with glossy print marks so that they are easier for beekeepers to find.

Some worker bees have the duty of being the water-carriers. They search for water sources, fill their crops by sipping as much water as they can, and return it to the hive. A hive needs about 1.5 gallons (5-6 litres) of water each day to stay cool in midsummer.

BEE-ing the Queen

Imagine being the queen bee. If you were the queen, you would be bigger than any of the other bees in your family—even the boy bees (the **drones**). That's because when you were little your sisters fed you royal jelly, a yellowish liquid secreted from worker bee heads.

Now that you're grown, you're the boss. You don't have to scrounge for food, build the hive, take care of the babies, or even clean yourself. Every bee in the colony does that work for you!

However, you do hold an important responsibility—you must lay all of the eggs in your nest or hive in order to keep your family thriving. You will lay nearly 1,500 eggs a day (during the warmer months) or about 1,500,000 eggs in your lifetime.

Cells opened to show queen larvae floating in royal jelly.

Who's in the Colony?

1. Queens: The queen's main job is to lay lots and lots of eggs.
2. Workers: These female bees are responsible for building, cleaning, and defending the nest, raising the babies, caring for the queen, foraging for food, and fanning the nectar.
3. Drones: The job of these male bees is simply to mate with the queen.

A honeycomb filled with eggs and larvae. All the sealed cells contain bee larvae.

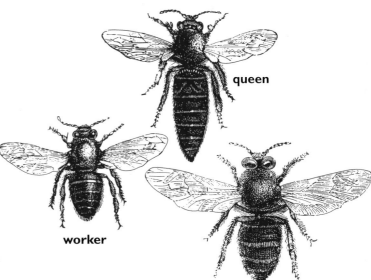

Honeybees

Do you have brothers or sisters? Imagine having 40,000-60,000 siblings (mostly sisters) living in the same home as you. Honeybees are social bees. They live together in large colonies, especially in the summer. In the winter months many honeybees die, leaving only a few thousand. Together, they keep warm by vibrating their bodies.

Sometimes colonies of bees outgrow their nests or hives, or worse, a predator such as a honey wasp, skunk, or bear invades. When this happens, honeybees have been known to swarm. The swarm can contain tens of thousands of worker bees—all following the queen. Beekeepers try to avoid swarms by rearranging or removing frames from the hive. These keepers do not want swarms since these evacuations usually result in the loss of their bees and ultimately the loss of precious honey.

Three Types of Honeybees

Domesticated European Honeybees *(Apis mellifera)*

Features

o Have barbed stingers, so they can only sting once
o Amber/brown and black
o Pollen baskets on legs
o Mild mannered

Stingless Bees *(Meliponines)*

Features

o Their stingers are non-functional and cannot pierce human skin
o Fuzzy bodies
o Stop moving when predators are near
o Nest in tree branches and hollow trees
o Shy nature

Giant Asian Honeybees *(Apis dorsata)*

Features

o Barbed stingers
o Bold bands of orange, black, and white
o Dark, transparent wings
o The length of your thumb
o Black fuzzy heads
o Gentle temperament

European honeybee

HONEY: Liquid Gold

Honeybees are not the only social bees to make honey. Bumblebees, for example, live together in small groups (between 50 and 100 bees) in grass-lined holes. These native North American bees also make, store, and feed on honey.

In some stingless-bee colonies, there may be a few egg-laying "queens" as well as groups of female worker bees all sharing the same nest. Stingless bees create small wax pods to store their honey. Stingless-bee honey is some of the tastiest honey in the world—some say it is worth its weight in gold!

Bumblebees

Like honeybees, bumblebees also make honey. However, humans shouldn't collect bumblebee honey for two reasons. First, unlike honeybees, bumblebees only store a few days' worth of food. Taking their honey would leave them vulnerable to food shortages. Second, to extract bumblebee honey, beekeepers would need to break into their nests, possibly destroying eggs and young larvae in the process.

WAGGLE DANCE

My sister is a worker bee.
We come from the same hive.
She leads us in the waggle dance
that keeps us all alive.

The way she moves her body
lets us know where we must go
to find the fields and gardens
where the finest flowers grow.

Her dancing is symmetrical—
A figure eight, I'd say.
The more wiggly she waggles,
the farther the bouquet.

Across a line of symmetry,
she dances equal sections—
making a map, whose two parts
are identical reflections.

She waggles in this mirrored way
to act as our director.
Now we know the route to fly
to bring home tasty nectar.

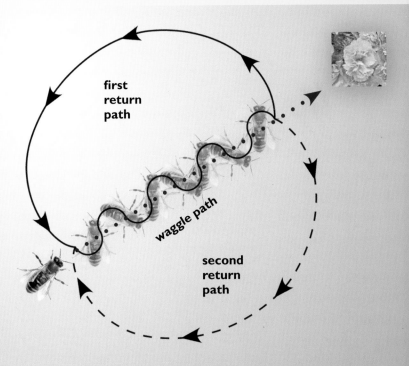

first
return
path

second
return
path

In addition to the danced communication, bees also send messages through chemical smells. For instance, crushed bees send out chemical messages using pheromones, warning their colonies of potential dangers.

Keeping BUZZ-y

Carpenter Bees

Beekeepers use wooden hives to house their bees. These hives have removable wooden frames placed inside to house the honeycomb.

Carpenter bees burrow holes into wooden structures like fence posts, old barns, and unpainted buildings.

Mining Bees

Mining bees are ground nesters. It is not uncommon for these shy medium-sized bees to excavate a tunnel the length of a pencil.

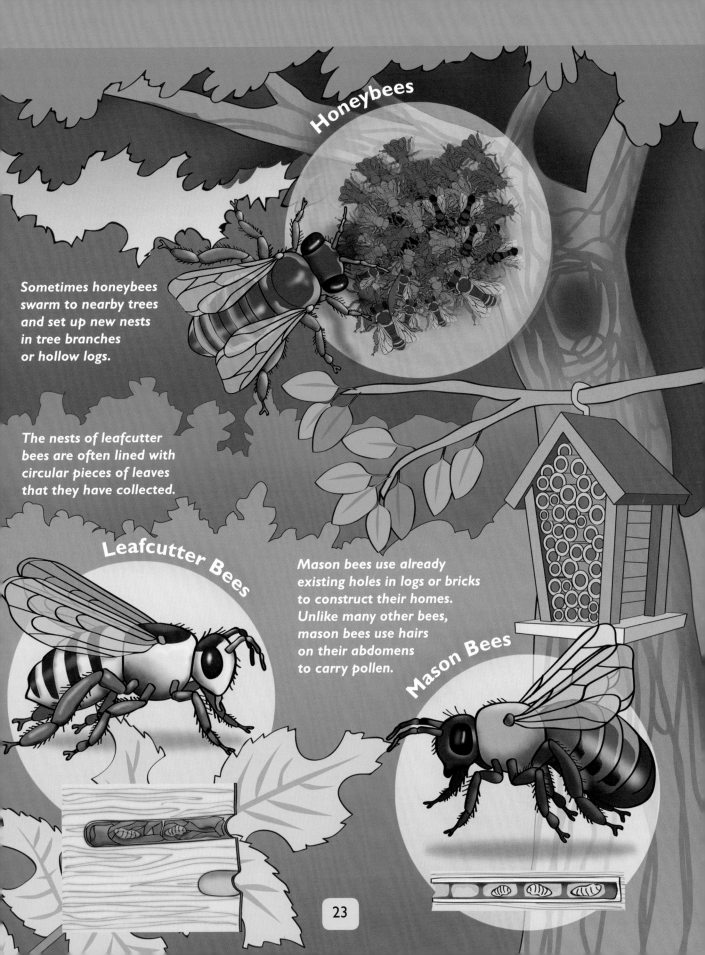

Honeybees

Sometimes honeybees swarm to nearby trees and set up new nests in tree branches or hollow logs.

The nests of leafcutter bees are often lined with circular pieces of leaves that they have collected.

Leafcutter Bees

Mason bees use already existing holes in logs or bricks to construct their homes. Unlike many other bees, mason bees use hairs on their abdomens to carry pollen.

Mason Bees

23

CHAPTER 4

BEE-ING ALONE

Not all bees live together. Some live by themselves or with only their babies in dirt holes amongst flowers, in flower-petal nests, or even inside wooden patio furniture or fence posts. In fact, the majority of bees worldwide are solitary (an estimated 97-99%), meaning they exist alone without a colony. These isolated insects often only communicate with other bees during mating season.

BEE-autiful Homes

Solitary bees, such as leafcutter bees, mason bees, and some carpenter bees, typically build nests in the ground, rotten logs, or plant stems. But none of these homes is as beautiful as the *osmia avosetta* bee's petal nest.

Researchers from both Turkey and Iran recently discovered this solitary bee building colourful and fragile cocoons from flowers. She is a hardworking bee that bites flower petals, flies them to her burrow, and then shapes a cocoon, petal by petal, using nectar to hold it together. After filling the bottom with **bee bread** (a mixture of nectar, pollen, and saliva), the *osmia avosetta* bee lays a single egg. Finally, she protects the egg by folding the cocoon's edges inward. Now that's a safe and beautiful home!

Living BEE-side Each Other

Some solitary bees live beside one another. An example of this living arrangement is demonstrated by blue orchard mason bees. These non-honey bees tend to choose locations near fruit-tree blossoms (their main food source). Evidence shows that with this

Mining bee

Although mining bees might live together (even sharing the same nest entrance), they do not help their neighbours raise the babies. In this case, imagine an apartment building, where groups of people can live at the same address, but might not know one another.

bee there is a relationship between the amount of food available and the number of eggs laid. In other words, more food = more babies. It is not uncommon to see 40-50 mother bees of this species living in groups, but wanting nothing to do with each other.

Unlike other solitary bees such as digger bees, orchard mason bees rely on other insects or creatures such as beetles or woodpeckers to drill holes for them, since they are not capable of making their own. These shy, non-aggressive bees will even live in human-made homes.

BEE-fore I Leave You

Orchard mason bees spend the winter inside a self-built waterproof cocoon, in a state of **torpor**—temporary hibernation. By spring, they need food and water. Since male eggs are placed closer to the chamber entrance, they emerge first. These boy bees chew away at the end of the cocoon and at the thick mud barrier that separates them from the outside. Once free from their tunnels, they stretch their wings, eat, and wait three to four days for the females to hatch. As the female waits for her wings to dry so she can visit and **pollinate** the flowers, the males mate with her. Soon after, the male mason bees die. Meanwhile the female gets busy eating and trying to locate a new nesting hole. Once she finds a hole, she marks it with a pheromone, a chemical which tells the other female bees that it has been taken. Then she looks for mud, pollen, and nectar to stuff in the tunnel. She positions herself on the sticky pile and then lays a translucent egg. Next, she finds more mud in order to create a circular chamber around her young. Over the next 30 days, she will lay 35-40 more eggs and protect each one with a mud shell. Soon after these four weeks, she will also die.

Many female solitary bees make excellent mothers. A mother dying of old age will work numerous hours by herself in order to create a proper home and provide bee bread for her babies.

Though woodpeckers help solitary bees make their homes—by drilling holes in wooden posts and trees—woodpeckers also eat bees.

ACTIVITY: Creating a Nesting Site for Orchard Mason Bees

Nesting sites can be drilled into untreated wooden blocks, or constructed by using clusters of soda straws inserted into a tin can. Let's look closer at this construction process. (You will need an adult to supervise and help you with this activity.)

1.

To create such a dwelling, follow the directions.

Step 1: Gather the following materials:
- 3 untreated wood blocks 10 x 15 in (25.5 x 38 cm), pine or fir. For a simpler version, just use a rectangular block of wood with a flat-top roof.
- Drill
- 1 drill bit $^5/_{16}$ inches
- 16 nails or screws
- Hammer or screwdriver
- 2 pieces of cedar shingle or thin wood, bigger than the block, for the roof.

Step 2: Screw 3 pre-cut blocks together.

Step 3: Draw a grid pattern on the front face.

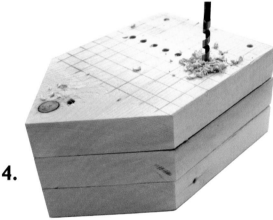

4.

Step 4: Drill holes
Drill holes $^3/_4$ inches apart. Be sure not to drill all the way through the wood.

Step 5: Roof
Attach the roof with nails or screws (do not use glue) to the top of the block. This will keep the bees shaded and dry.

Step 6: Mounting panel
Attach a vertical strip of wood at the back of the nest. This will help in hanging the nest from a tree or fence.

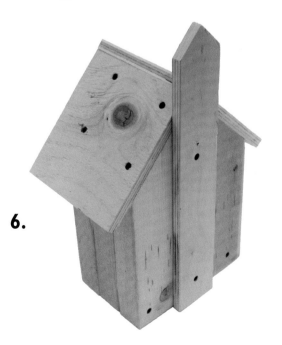

6.

Step 7: Hanging the nest
Drive a nail into a post, wooden fence or tree trunk. Secure the block firmly. Remember, these bees prefer to face east or south so that the morning warms them.

2.

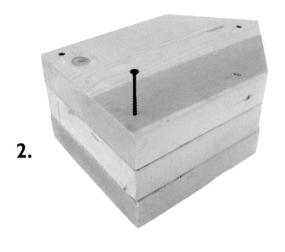

3.

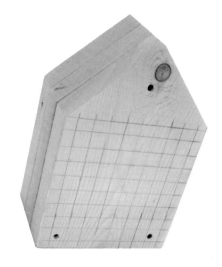

5.

7.

Getting BEE-gger

In early June, inside their secure nesting chambers called **galleries** (perhaps inside your deck or fence), carpenter bee eggs are hatching tiny grub-like larvae. These larvae eat the bee bread their mom has left for them. For nearly three weeks, the larvae move only a little. Mostly they just eat and eat, gathering strength for their upcoming bodily changes.

Carpenter bees spend the next three to four weeks (the pupa stage of their lives) inside their chambers, separated from their siblings by cell walls. Then in late summer, the adult carpenter bees will emerge to seek pollen and a mate. Soon after mating the male bees will die. Until the winter comes, the solitary females will spend the rest of their lives collecting nectar and pollen, and building nests for their own babies, before over-wintering (similar to hibernating). Mother carpenter bees may live another summer, but will die by the end of fall. It is very unlikely for a mother carpenter bee to live for two winters.

Carpenter bees are excellent mothers. For its baby's complete development, a mother carpenter bee will forage for twenty trips, collecting three times its own weight in pollen and nectar.

Carpenter bee

Life Cycle of a Bee

Adult bee
The adult bee emerges from the honeycomb about 15 to 24 days after the eggs are laid.

Eggs
The queen bee lays individual eggs in the cells of the honeycomb.

Pupae
Pupae develop from the larvae and begin growing all the adult body parts.

Queen bee

Larvae
Larvae hatch from the fertilized eggs in 3 days and are then fed by the worker bees.

BEES OF THE WORLD, DISPERSE!

Today, it is estimated that there are 19,500 species of bees found all over the world, on all continents but Antarctica. Some of these bees migrated on their own to new continents, while others were brought by people. Honeybees, for example, are not native to North America. European settlers within the last few hundred years brought these domesticated bees to Canada and the United States.

Bee Mobility

Bees can sense when an environment has been negatively influenced by humans. They will leave an area that is overdeveloped and not ecologically friendly.

Some bees are more mobile than others. The more mobile a species, the more likely it is to survive climate changes and other environmental difficulties. This is because mobile bees are able to move to areas where the conditions are more suitable for their specific needs. In general, the larger the bee, the more likely it is to be able to travel greater distances.

Being mobile uses a lot of energy. This means that commuting (travelling) bees have less energy available for collecting food and pollinating plants. If the commutes become too long or difficult, bees may not have enough food for their babies and their populations may decline.

Bee scientist Martin Wikelski has pioneered a miniature tracking tag that fits on the backs of bees. This monitoring device allows his research teams to study the flight pattern of bees.

Invasive Pests

Some bees migrate or are brought to new places, causing negative effects on their new environments. For example, the giant resin bee, a native of Asia, was accidentally brought to the United States in the 1990s and was identified in North Carolina in 1994. These large bees are sometimes considered pests.

A male Eastern carpenter bee (native to North America) visits a kudzu flower.

First, they compete with native bees (wild bees) for nesting sites, and second, they tend to pollinate invasive weeds such as kudzu, which crowds out and kills important native plants. Native bees are negatively affected because they find themselves with fewer food sources.

Killer Bees

In the 1950s, a Brazilian bee biologist named Warwick Kerr crossbred aggressive Africanized honeybees with hardworking Brazilian honeybees (which were originally from Europe). His hope was to create more peaceful, productive bees. The experiment backfired, however, when the "killer bees" (also known as Africanized bees) escaped, freed into Central America and Mexico. These aggressive and determined hybrids have proven to be more difficult to manage than other honeybee strains. They tend to swarm with greater frequency and to migrate when their food sources dwindle. Africanized bees aggressively guard their hives by positioning a greater number of guards and deploying bigger armies when they feel threatened. By 2003, this destructive bee strain had spread into the US.

There are three main economic problems that this bee migration caused:

1. Killer bees compete with the more domesticated North American/European bees for valuable resources like food, water, and mates.

2. Killer bees are harder to contain since they are quick to swarm when provoked. This means that beekeepers need to spend more time managing the hives.

3. Killer bees have more difficulty surviving the harsh winters. These colonies are less productive since they do not begin pollinating until later in the spring season.

Leave Me BEE Game

Instructions:

1. With the exception of two or three participants, all children find a partner.

2. Partners stand together. They join hands and face one another, creating a hive.

3. One of the two or three children without partners becomes a bee predator (e.g., a wasp, a bear, or a skunk). He/she chases the other single child/children (the bee/s).

4. These single participants must find safety from the predator by going inside a hive and joining hands with one of the partners.

5. The child who is behind the couple (the one left without hands to hold) can now be chased by the bee predator.

6. If the bee predator catches someone, he/she becomes "it" (the new predator).

The BEE's Knees

Imagine a world without bees. Not only would it be less colourful—with fewer wildflowers and flowering plants—it would be less fruitful too. A world without bees means a world where the food supply would be significantly diminished.

Canadian professor and global bee researcher Laurence Packer (2010) estimates that bees are responsible for one third of our food supply. He offers an activity as a way for people to think about the significance of these furry and valuable insects. The "BEE a Researcher" game is an adaptation of Packer's "Consider Breakfast, Then Thank a Bee" activity.

BEE a Researcher

Here is a lunch not uncommon to North Americans: a chicken Caesar wrap, carrot sticks, and a fruit smoothie.

Step 1: Think carefully about the food in this picture. Which foods would be unavailable if bees disappeared?

Step 2: Go to pages 44-45 and see if you guessed right!

Sweat Bees

Sweat bees are attracted to the salts found in human perspiration. A research study noted that some sweat bees have been known to sip people's tears. Imagine being sad, and while you are crying, a sweat bee lands on your cheek, rolls out its slender, hairy tongue (proboscis), and drinks your tears!

Though bees are efficient pollinators, bats, butterflies, humming birds, and moths can also pollinate plants.

Meal Item with Ingredients

Fruit Smoothie
- Watermelon
- Strawberries
- Honey

Caesar Wrap
- Whole wheat wrap
- Chicken
- Parmesan cheese
- Lettuce
- Tomato
- Caesar dressing
- Carrot sticks

Let Me BEE: I'm **BUZZ**-y Working

Humans need bees to pollinate plants. But what is it about bees that make them such good pollinators?

Some bees can visit thousands of flowers each day in order to collect their own food (e.g., nectar, pollen). Their hairy legs and bodies pick up flower particles called pollen. They also drop some of these tiny particles onto new flowers. This means that bees have the potential to pollinate hundreds of flowers every day. When a flower's egg comes in contact with pollen, there is a chance that it will grow into a seed.

Many plants depend on bees to pollinate their flowers in order to make new seeds. In fact, bees pollinate 87 of the world's 115 most important food crops. According to some, the estimated worth for the contribution of bees worldwide may be as high as $90 billion a year. For others, their contribution is priceless because the work they do keeps humans and animals alive— it's a matter of survival!

So the next time that you see a bee buzzing from flower to flower, please do not hurt it. Remember to just let it be because it is busy pollinating the world's flowers and food supply.

BEE-ing a Beekeeper

While some people see bees as scary or as pests, others see them as helpful or even as pets. In the eyes of a **bee handler**, bees are seen as special, even heroic, because the lives of many creatures depend on them.

People who raise or take care of bees are called beekeepers or bee handlers. Some beekeepers raise and care for honeybees. They may sell the bees' honey or products made from beeswax.

Glen McMullen is one of these people. He and his wife, Gwen, keep honeybees and sell bee products (e.g., honey, honeycomb, beeswax). At the same time, by keeping bees safe, they are helping all of us because they are helping the farms in their area grow healthier crops.

Glen says, "For me, the greatest thrill of all is to go to the bee yard and lift up the top and see that we have a strong hive; there's an immense amount of satisfaction and joy in finding a thriving, active hive."

Beekeepers need to practise responsible beekeeping (i.e., not taking too much honey) if they want their colonies to thrive.

Some beekeepers, like Glen, rent out their honeybees to other farmers in order to pollinate more fields.

Still other bee handlers keep other types of bees. For example, Paul and Maude Stephany keep mason bees. They write, "We found out that mason bees are docile, that they rarely sting, and that their venom is very mild compared to other bees. Indeed, in the more than four years that we've been keeping mason bees, we have yet to get stung! Which is amazing considering that we often stand right next to their tubes while they're busy collecting pollen...all they do is buzz close to us and look our way."

Additionally, they chose mason bees because they knew that there are many challenges facing wild pollinators, such as declining populations. By raising mason bees, they released many of these native bees back into their natural environments, enabling them to thrive once more.

A beekeeper prepares a smoker by stuffing paper and cardboard into the canister and lighting it.

The smoke will make the bees drowsy and less active.

Once the frames are removed, the beekeeper can gently inspect the combs or extract honey without harming the bees.

Right: Author Kari-Lynn Winters experiences the job of a beekeeper first-hand.

A SWEET Life

Besides the pollen that collects on their furry bodies or in their pollen baskets, some bees also collect nectar from flowers.

Honeybees take in this sweet liquid through their straw-like tongues. For a short time the nectar is stored in their honey stomachs until they can get back to their nest or hive. Once in their homes, the honeybees regurgitate the nectar from their honey stomachs, pass it from bee to bee, and then spit it into the wax cells, all the while mixing it with enzymes from their heads and mouths. Then to make the nectar less runny, they fan it with their wings. The moving air helps the excessive water in the nectar to evaporate. The cell is then capped with beeswax. Honeybees save this stored nectar or honey to help them survive during the winter months. Beekeepers collect excess honey by slicing off the caps with a thin honey knife and spinning the combs in a machine called an extractor.

Honeybees visit nearly 1,000,000 flowers in order to create one pound of honey.

CHAPTER 6

STINGING EFFECTS ON THE WORLD

The world as we know it would be very different without bees. Not only would there be significantly fewer flowers and foods, there would be fewer predators—both bee predators and predators of other species that depend on flowering plants. In addition to the bee predators (e.g., wasps, woodpeckers, bears, skunks, lizards, dragonflies), predators of these vegetarian animals, like wolves, foxes, eagles, and weasels would also be affected. Indeed, the disappearance of bees would have stinging effects on food webs around the globe.

We need bees. As Albert Einstein once stated, "If bees disappeared, humans would have only 4 years left to live."

BEE-hind the Eight Ball

Colony Collapse Disorder

Since 1945 there has been a continuous decline in the number of honeybees worldwide. This decline has intensified in recent years; in fact, many beekeepers from across North America are reporting that several of their bee colonies have disappeared. The syndrome, which describes a mass disappearance of bees, is called **colony collapse disorder** (CCD). What is most disturbing about these colony collapses is that they were not caused by the usual invasion of honey raiders such as bears, beetles, skunks, or wasps. Rather, these bees had simply vanished! Newspapers like the *New York Times* state that, since 2006, 20%-40% of bee colonies in the United States alone have suffered from colony collapse. Countries such as Japan, China, Egypt, and Canada have also been affected by collapses in their honeybee colonies. The worldwide collapses pose a major threat to farming economies and to global food production.

BEE-coming Extinct

Around the world, there is mounting evidence that non-domesticated bees are also disappearing at an alarming rate, including bumblebees, alkali bees, mason bees, and sweat bees. For example, researchers in the US have noticed that four species of bumblebees have declined by 96%. This is important as bumblebees are the prime pollinators of blueberries, cranberries, and tomatoes, as well as other native plants. British researchers discovered that three of their fifty bumblebee species are now extinct, while ten are still in danger and could disappear over the next five years. Reports from India and Canada suggest similar results—that various solitary bees from these countries are disappearing.

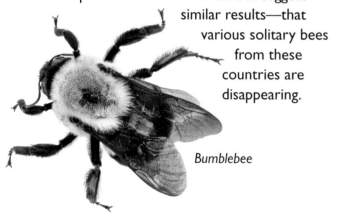

Bumblebee

What's the BUZZ?
Tell Me What's Happening!

Though many possible explanations of CCD have been proposed by scientists, no one explanation has been agreed upon. Rather, causes of bee declines may relate to a number of factors: disease caused by bacterial, viral and fungal infections, parasites, pesticides and pollution, shrinking habitats, climate changes, and even an unbalanced diet.

Disease: Bacterial, Viral, and Fungal Infections

American bee researcher Diana Cox-Foster suggests that a virus called the Israeli acute paralysis virus (IAPV), a disease that destroys bees' digestive tracts, deserves further investigation. Although the virus was detected in nearly all the CCD colonies that were researched, there is still no proof that this virus caused CCD.

Viral and fungal infections may be another reason why the bees are dying. Researchers at the University of Montana found that a combination of a viral infection (insect iridescent) and a fungal parasite (**Nosema**) were discovered in several honeybees affected by the colony collapse. These

researchers think that a similar viral infection may have wiped out bee populations in India nearly 20 years ago.

Parasites

Two types of parasites have been found in dying bee colonies. The first are called **tracheal mites**. These parasites live in the breathing tubes of bees. Imagine having cockroaches in your lungs—these large mites have crippling effects on bees, making it hard for them to breathe. Because these mites are inside the bees' bodies, they can be difficult to detect.

The second parasite is called the **varroa mite**. Imagine having a mosquito on your back, but one the size of a backpack.

A recent research study suggests that a parasitic fly, nicknamed a "zombie fly," has been discovered laying eggs inside bee abdomens. As the hatching larvae push their way out of the bee between its thorax and abdomen, the bee dies.

These destructive bloodsuckers latch on to the bees, using the bees' blood for nourishment.

Though mites cause damage to hives, some researchers have shown that mites do not appear to be the primary cause of CCD.

Pesticides and Pollution

Pesticides are usually sprayed on plants for weed control and to kill insects and bugs that may harm the plants. However, bees are insects too. So the same pesticides that keep our crops pest-free might also be the poisons that are killing the bees. In other words, exposure to pesticides and air pollution may have accidentally killed some bees, or it may have left bees more vulnerable to viral and bacterial infections.

Shrinking Habitats

Around the globe, natural habitats are being taken over and turned into houses, factories, restaurants, malls and parking lots. These growing, human-made spaces impact the insects, birds, and animals that depend on the natural environment for their survival. Fewer forests and meadows mean fewer trees and flowers, which means fewer food sources for bees and other wildlife.

Varroa mites attach themselves to bees and drink their blood.

Climate Changes

Variations in temperature and precipitation (rain and snow) have the potential to affect bees. Though bees can withstand cold temperatures by huddling together and shivering their wings, cold temperatures mixed with wet conditions can be a deadly combination for bees.

Unbalanced Diets

Blueberries are good for you. They are rich in vitamin C and dietary fibre and are powerful antioxidants, meaning they have the potential to reduce the risk of stroke and cancer. However, if all you ate were blueberries for months at a time—for breakfast, lunch, dinner, and snacks—you might not feel healthy and you might be more susceptible to disease. The same is true with honeybees. Since bees are efficient pollinators, honeybees are transported across the United States and Canada in order to do the pollinating. This means that bees may have unbalanced diets. For example, they might only sip almond nectar in March and April, citrus nectar in May, blueberry nectar in June, and pumpkin nectar in August. The lack of variety in their diets can weaken their immune systems or make them sick.

BEE the Change the World Needs

Humans rely on bees. It's not too late to make a difference. Kids and adults alike can make simple changes in their lives to help bees.

1. BEE-come Educated

Pay attention to bees and their environments. Study them. Share your expertise with others. For example, if you see someone swatting a bee, tell them that most bees are not aggressive and will only sting when they need to protect themselves or their colonies. Remind them that we need bees to pollinate many of the foods we eat and that many other animals rely on bees too.

Most of the world's bees are simply friendly insects that just want to be left alone. Wild bees often can be observed minding their own business, collecting food for their **brood** and busily building their nests in ground holes, gaps in dead wood, or in the hollows of trees. They won't bother you unless you bother them.

4. Provide Water for Surv-HIVE-al

Like all living creatures, bees need water to survive. Put out shallow bowls of water. Put rocks in the bowl so that the bees have a place to land.

5. HONEY, Please Pass the Honey

Honey tastes great and it is good for you too. Honey is better than sugar because it is rich in vitamins, minerals, and healthy enzymes. Support local beekeepers and local bees by buying and eating local honey. And after you are done eating, be sure to tell your friends about how good local honey tastes.

2. BEE-ware of Toxic Seeds

Some seeds have been coated with insecticides such as Clothianidin. These chemicals are toxic to bees. Be sure to ask your parents to buy seeds that are insecticide-free.

3. Create a Backyard BUZZ

Create a backyard buzz with a wild bee garden. These gardens, when planted with native plants that bloom successively from spring to fall, can provide nourishment and safe havens for local bees throughout the year. Research has shown that bees prefer messier gardens with 10 or more species planted together. Consider planting some open-faced flowers such as aster, saskatoon, or stone-crop.

6. Let Fruits and Veggies BEE

Let vegetable plants "bolt" or go to seed. For example, the blue and purple flowers of lettuce plants can provide pollen for bees during the fall and winter months. The hollow stems of raspberry or elderberry canes can provide nesting material or homes for solitary bees.

You can make your own bee home from a tin can filled with bamboo canes. Drill out the pith to make the holes large enough.

7. Build Your Own BEE Home

Mason bees and carpenter bees prefer to live and lay eggs inside wooden tunnels. Untreated wooden blocks with drilled holes can be mounted in your yard.

8. Create Cell Phone-Free BEE Zones

There have been scientific reports that suggest radiation given off from cell phones has the potential to interfere with a bee's navigation system. Other reports have disputed this information. Regardless, why not create a cell phone-free zone in your backyard? Post signs and ask people not to use cell phones in that area.

9. BEE-Friendly, Buy Organic

Some pesticides are toxic to bees. Buying organic, pesticide-free foods supports farmers who are growing bee-friendly foods.

10. BEE Involved

Create "Save the BEE" signs and post them outside your home. Talk to your teachers. Ask if you might be able to do a unit on bees. Write letters to government officials. Educate everyone you know about the importance of bees.

Mason bee

Answer Key for "BEE a Researcher" Activity (pages 32-33)

Would these foods be available if bees disappeared?

Meal Item with Ingredients	Affected Foods
Caesar Wrap	Yes. Wheat is mostly pollinated by the wind.
Whole wheat wrap **Chicken**	To some extent. Although chicken feed is primarily made up of corn, oats, and soybeans, all of which are wind pollinated, free-range chickens also eat greens, veggie parings, and insects. Many of these items depend upon bee pollination.
Parmesan cheese	To some extent. Cheese is typically made from cow's milk Cows eat grasses, alfalfa, clover, and silage (fermented grass). Though some grass pollens are blown by the wind, pollination by honeybees bumblebees, and leafcutter bees is essential for alfalfa seed production. Clover would not exist if bees did not pollinate it.
Lettuce	Yes. Lettuce self-pollinates.
Tomatoes	No. Crops that produce fruit (such as tomatoes or sweet peas) need to be pollinated in order for the fruit to develop.
Caesar dressing	To some extent. Like cheese, Caesar dressing is typically made from milk products. Often these are made from cow's milk (see Parmesan cheese).
Carrot Sticks	
Carrots	Yes. Carrots are pollinated by bees.

Fruit Smoothie

Watermelon

No. Watermelons are entirely dependent on bee pollination.

Strawberries

No. Strawberries need bees in order to produce fruit.

Honey

No. Without bees, there would be no honey.

Yogurt

To some extent. Again, yogurt is typically made from cow's milk (see Parmesan cheese).

Orange juice

No. Oranges (and at least seven other foods that provide vitamin C) depend on bee pollination.

Glossary

Bee Bread: Some bees feed their babies bee bread—a mixture of nectar, pollen, and saliva.

Bee Handler: Someone who raises or takes care of bees.

Beeswax: A flaky substance secreted and used by some bees to build their brood structures and to store their food. Beeswax is also melted and used by humans to create commercial products like candles, shoe polish, and lip gloss.

Brood: Bee babies.

Colony Collapse Disorder (CCD): A syndrome that describes the mass disappearance of thousands of bees worldwide.

Compound Eyes: These two larger eyes are made up of over 6,900 minute hexagons, helping the bee see all around its body.

Drones: Male bees.

Galleries: Tunnel-like habitats where solitary bees nest.

Hieroglyphics: A formal writing system used 5,000 years ago in Egypt.

Honeycomb: A mass of hexagon cells found inside a honeybee's hive or nest.

Honey Hunter: An occupation in pre-historic times where brave men would climb extremely high and flimsy ladders in order to collect tangy honey from wild bees for their tribes.

Mead: Fermented honey water.

Nosema: A fungal parasite that sometimes affects honeybee colonies.

Ocelli: Three smaller eyes—which detect light—located between the bee's antennae.

Pheromones: Chemicals created or sensed by bees to signal danger, to detect food sources, and to attract mates.

Pollination: The fertilization of a flowering plant.

Pollen Baskets: Only found on some bees, these concave areas of the hind legs are fringed by stiff hairs, and used to transport pollen from the flower to the hive.

Propolis: A tree resin collected by bees.

Proboscis: A straw-like tongue, used by bees to sip nectar and feed their babies. Bee proboscises vary in length, determining which flowers they can eat from.

Scopa: Stiff hairs found on the hind legs of some bees. Like pollen baskets, these hairs are used to transport pollen from the flower to the hive.

Social Bees: These bees depend on their colonies to survive. Social bees work together, and take care of their colony's babies, and queen. Only a few of the females in these social groups lay eggs.

Solitary Bees: These bees survive without a colony to depend on.

Thorax: The middle section of an insect's body. The bee's six legs and four wings are attached to its thorax.

Torpor: Temporary hibernation.

Tracheal Mites: Parasites that block the tracheal tubes of bees.

Varroa Mites: Parasites that attach themselves to the backs of bees.

Index

Further Reading on Bees

Teacher's Guide
http://www.fitzhenry.ca/Download/guides/
BuzzAboutBeesTeachersGuide.doc

Online Resources
http://www.fitzhenry.ca/BuzzAboutBees

Reference List

Buchmann, S. (2006). *Letters from the hive*. New York: Bantam.

Fisher, R. (2010). *Bee*. New York: Princeton Architectural Press.

Griffin, B. (1993). *The Orchard mason bee*. Bellingham, WA: Knox Cedars Publishing.

Packer, L. (2010). *Keeping the bees: Why all bees are at risk and what we can do to save them*. Toronto: Harper Collins.

Pundyk, G. (2008). *The honey trail*. New York: St. Marten's Press.

Winston, M. (1987). *The biology of the honey bee*. Cambridge, MA: Harvard University Press.

Other Book Resources for Children

Burns, L. (2010). *The hive detectives: Chronicle of a honey bee catastrophe*. New York: Houghton Mifflin Harcourt.

Cole, J. & Degen, B. (1996). *The magic school bus: Inside a beehive*. New York: Scholastic Press.

Howard, F. (2005). *Bumble bees*. Mankato, MN: Capstone Press.

Rotner, S. & Woodhull, A. (2010). *The buzz on bees: Why are they disappearing?* New York: Holiday House.

Photo and Illustration Credits

Photographs

Alarob—page 30

Bauer, Scott (USDA Agricultural Research Service)—pages 18, 45 (orange juice)

Bubbs, Jenny—page 31

Garvey, Kathy Keatley/Fishback, Brian—page 40 (bee beard)

Hiemstra, Christy (Clovermead)—page 3

Huang, Zachary—page 9 (plates)

Intropin—page 11 (EpiPen)

Istock—pages 3 (bee photographs), 5, 6 (bees and scroll), 7, 10 (bee face and eyes), 12 (legs), 15, 21 (honeycomb), 32 (bird), 44-45 (bee)

Luckhurst, John—pages 3 (nesting site), 8 (candles), 17 (tree), 26-27, 32-33 (fruits and vegetables), 41 (seeds, flower basket), 42 (sticks and canes), 44-45 (food)

Merdal—page 17 (honeycomb)

Paonessa, Francesco—pages 8 (lip balm, tea), 11 (screw and nail), 32-33 (smoothie, wrap, carrots), 41 (bowl of rocks)

Sandusky, Cathy—pages 16 (honeycomb with bees), 17 (box hive), 34-35, 36

Shutterstock—pages 8 (wax), 38 (bumblebee) to "Shutterstock—pages 8 (wax), 16 (honeybee), 19 (bee comparison), 24-25 (log), 34 (sunflowers and bee), 38 (bumblebee)

Sullivan, John—page 37

Tubby, Ben—page 25 (woodpecker)

USDA—pages 37-38 (varroa mites)

Waugsberg—pages 11 (bee sting), 19 (royal jelly eggs and honeycomb larvae)

Winters, Kari-Lynn—page 42 (save the bee protest)

Wysotski, David (Allure Illustrations)—pages 1, 12 (honeybee), 14, 24 (mining bee), 28, 43

Illustrations

Clark, Warren—pages 3 (anatomy illustration), 9 (anatomy illustration), 22-23

Foord, Toby—pages 12 (wing illustration), 21 (waggle dance illustration)

Luckhurst, John—page 7 (hieroglyph)

Paonessa, Francesco and Gokool, Richard—page 29 (life cycle)

Sandusky, Cathy—page 7 (coin)